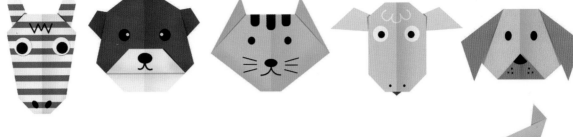

THIS BOOK
BELONGS TO

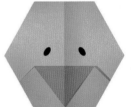

....

....

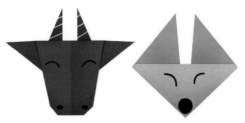

The start of the story

When Mom learned that I was on the way
_____

_____

_____

_____

What Mom said to Dad
_____

_____

How Dad reacted
_____

_____

While she was waiting for me, Mom imagined me like this
_____

_____

_____

_____

_____

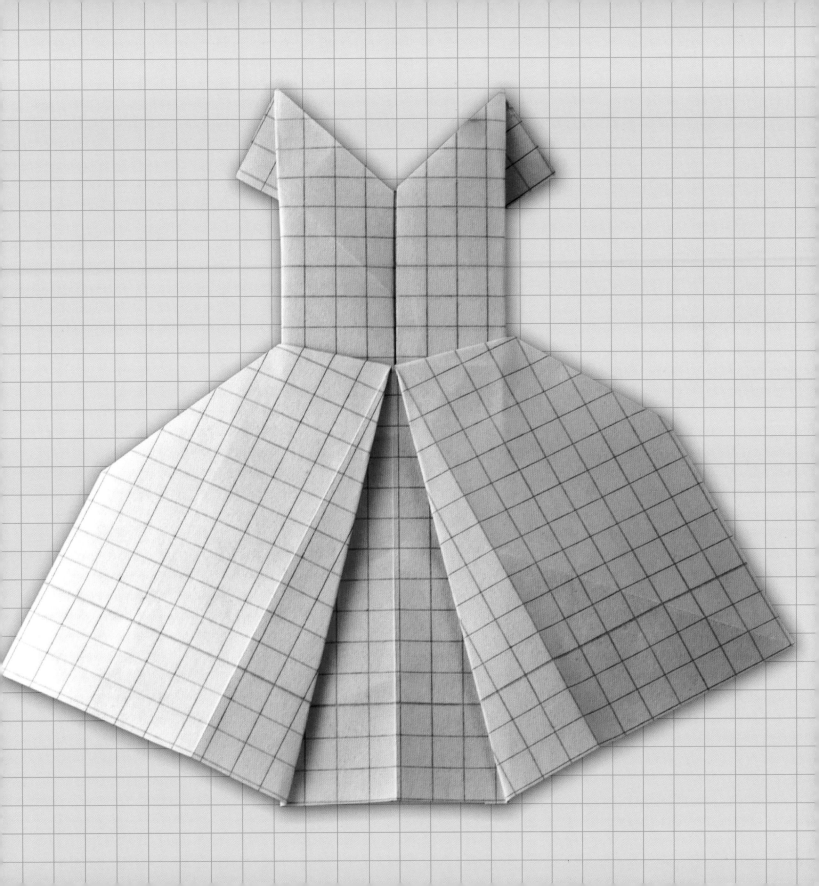

In Mom's big tummy

My parents heard my heartbeat for the first time

_____

_____

_____

Mom felt me kick for the first time

_____

_____

_____

While waiting for me, Mom always had a craving for

_____

_____

_____

My family made important preparations before my arrival, such as

_____

_____

_____

The First Sonogram

My family

Mom's name is
_____

Her dream for me is
_____
_____
_____
_____

Dad's name is
_____

His dream for me is
_____
_____
_____

The other members of my family

My family tree

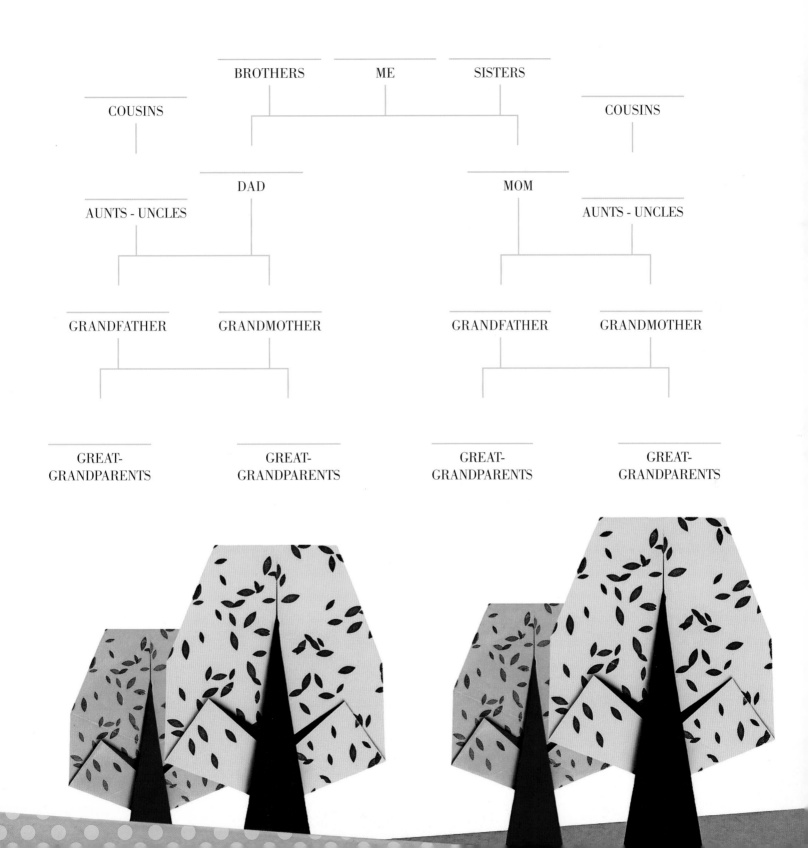

BROTHERS   ME   SISTERS

COUSINS   COUSINS

DAD   MOM

AUNTS - UNCLES   AUNTS - UNCLES

GRANDFATHER   GRANDMOTHER   GRANDFATHER   GRANDMOTHER

GREAT-
GRANDPARENTS   GREAT-
GRANDPARENTS   GREAT-
GRANDPARENTS   GREAT-
GRANDPARENTS

Family photos

Here I am!

I was born on

At

My weight

My height

I came into the world at

The doctor and obstetrician in attendance were

Mom and Dad describe my first day like this

My photos

What they said about me...

Mom's first words were

_____

_____

_____

_____

_____

Dad's first words were

_____

_____

_____

_____

The reactions of my siblings, cousins, grandparents, uncles,

aunts and friends

_____

_____

_____

I also received best wishes from

_____

_____

Precious mementos

A lock of my hair

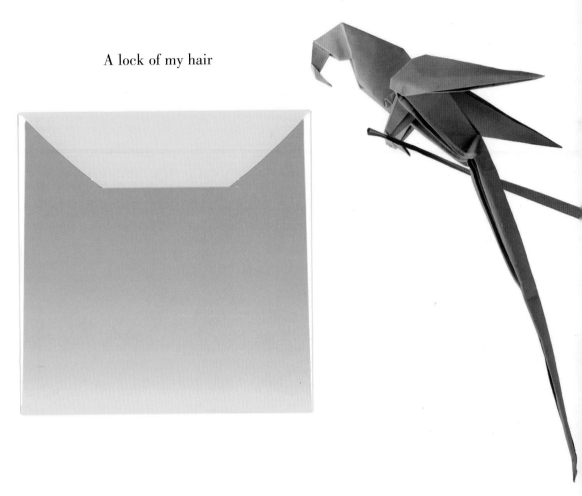

My hospital's bracelet

My name

Mom's and Dad's favorite names were

_____

_____

_____

The name they decided on is _____

They chose this name because _____

_____

_____

My name means _____

_____

_____

My nickname is _____

They call me in this way because _____

_____

My identikit

My eyes _____

My hair _____

My skin color _____

_____

What I got from Mom _____

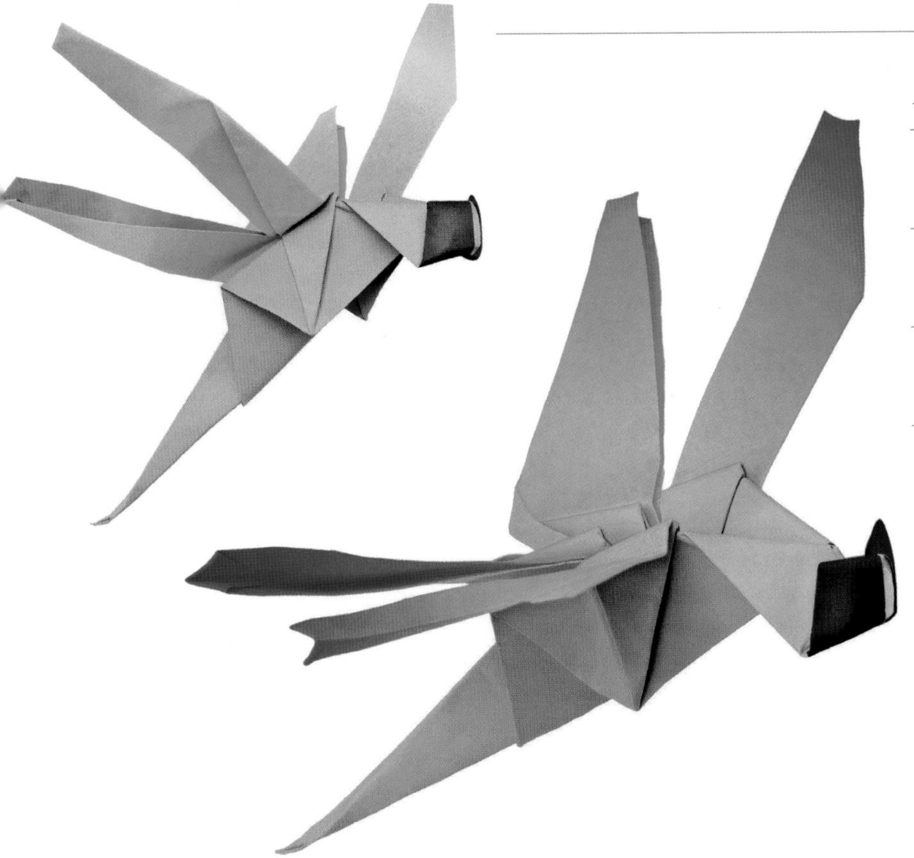

_____

What I got from Dad _____

_____

_____

_____

My photos

Home at last!

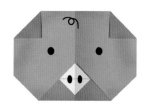

The date I arrived at home

My first address

During the trip, I

Waiting for me at home

As soon as I was inside, I

My bedroom is decorated like this

Around me were gifts from persons dear to me

My photos

Sweet dreams!

My first night at home I slept _____ hours
_____

And my parents slept _____ hours
_____

That first night they thought
_____

_____

_____

To fall asleep I need
_____

_____

_____

My favorite lullaby is
_____

_____

_____

_____

The position I sleep in

I can't fall asleep if

Wake up, sleepyhead!

Am I an early riser or a sleepyhead?

_____

_____

_____

_____

This is how I tell everyone I'm awake

_____

_____

_____

_____

As soon as I open my eyes, I immediately want

_____

_____

_____

_____

_____

My photos

It's time to eat!

My first solid food _____

_____

_____

_____

Mom's recipes _____

_____

_____

_____

_____

My favorite dish _____

_____

_____

_____

I really don't like _____

_____

_____

_____

_____

_____

I used a spoon all by myself when I was _____

_____

_____

It's bath time

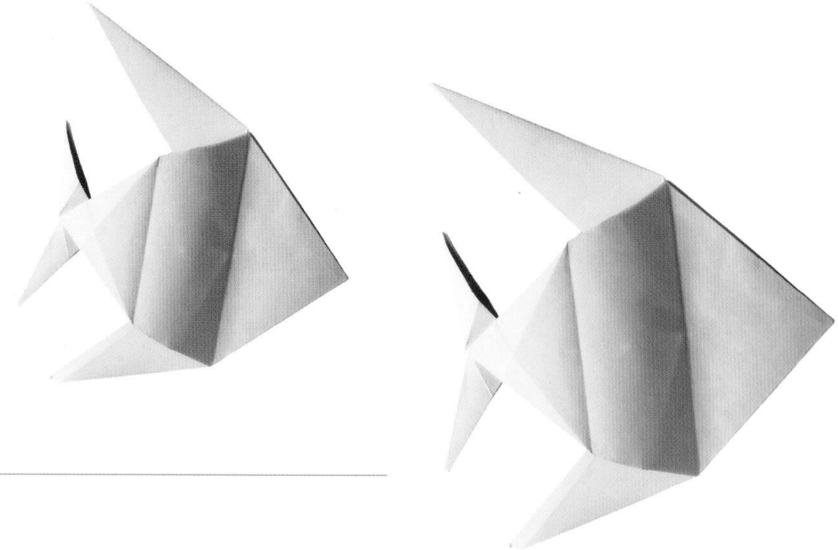

My first time in water

My reactions

In the water I enjoy

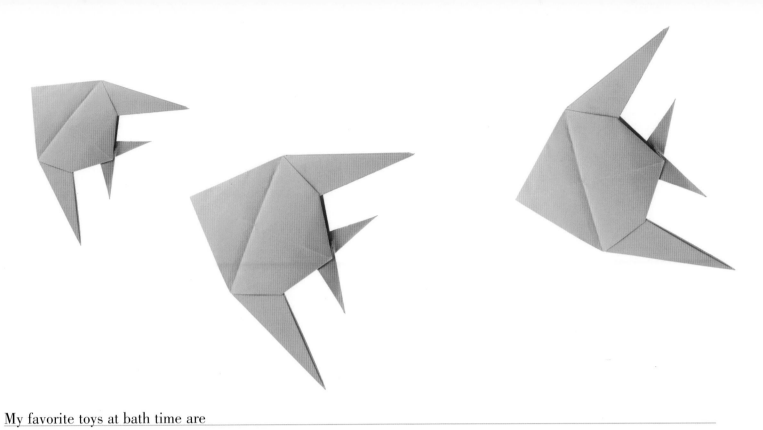

My favorite toys at bath time are

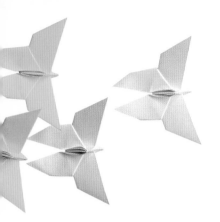

My photos

My development stages

	Weight	Height	Head circumference
At birth			
One month			
Two months			
Three months			
Four months			
Five months			
Six months			
Seven months			
Eight months			
Nine months			
Ten months			
Eleven months			
Twelve months			
Two years			
Three years			

Vaccinations

Baby teeth - At the doctor

central incisor

lateral incisor

canine

first molar

second molar

upper jaw

LEFT PROFILE

RIGHT PROFILE

lower jaw

second molar

first molar

canine

lateral incisor

central incisor

central incisor

lateral incisor

canine

first molar

second molar

second molar

first molar

canine

lateral incisor

central incisor

My pediatrician

During my first visit I

My blood group

The first time that I was sick

39

Discovering the world!

The first family stroll was

This was my reaction

The persons I met said the following about me

My favorite places are

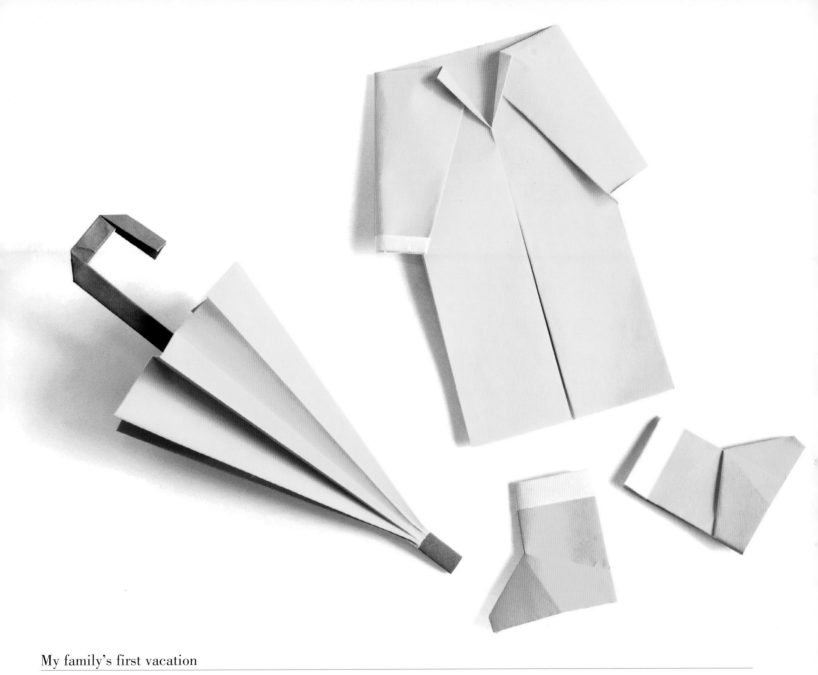

My family's first vacation

_____

_____

_____

_____

My photos

My first steps

I started crawling

I stood up on my own

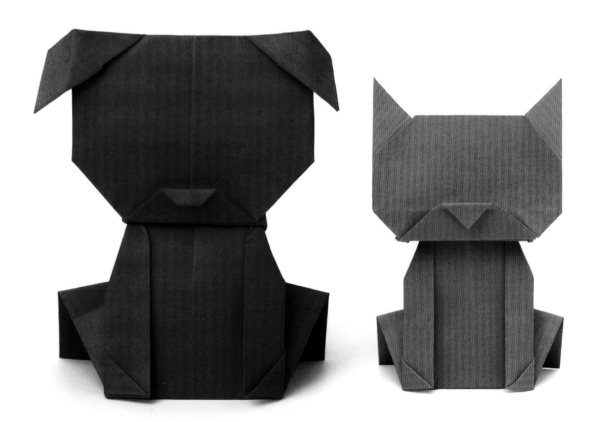

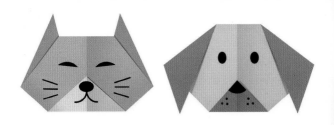

I took my first steps with a little help

_____

_____

_____

_____

I walked on my own for the first time

_____

_____

_____

_____

I tried running

_____

_____

_____

_____

_____

A special occasion

The event

_____

_____

_____

_____

Who was there

_____

_____

_____

_____

How I behaved

_____

_____

_____

_____

_____

_____

An unforgettable memory

_____

_____

_____

_____

_____

_____

My photos

My first birthday

The guests

The cake

The gifts

My favorite gift

Memories of the party

My photos

The first time that

I built a tower

I tried to get dressed on my own

I ate on my own

I threw a ball in the air

I jumped

A new experience

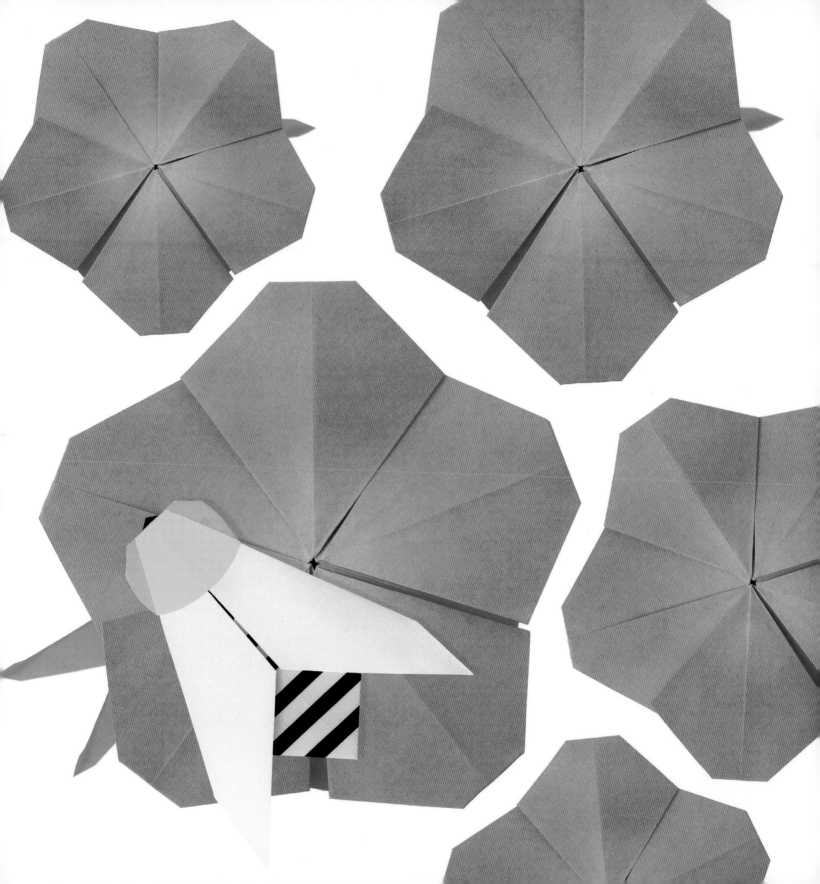

My first words

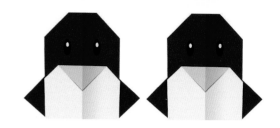

My first word was
_____

_____

I said it
_____

_____

_____

I said "Mom" for the first time
_____

_____

_____

I said "Dad" for the first time
_____

_____

_____

_____

_____

My favorites

My favorite book

The toy I never get bored with

I smile every time I hear this song

I like playing these games with Mom and Dad

The thing that makes me happier than anything else

The thing that makes me angrier than anything else

What consoles me

On vacation

Our destination

_____

_____

_____

_____

How I behaved

_____

_____

_____

_____

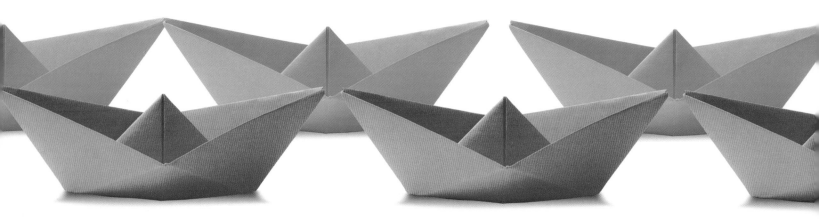

An unforgettable memory

_____

_____

_____

_____

_____

_____

_____

_____

_____

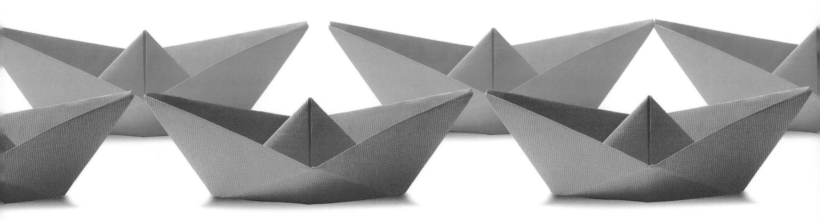

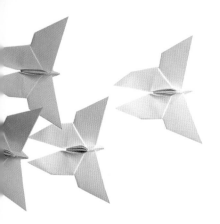

My photos

My second birthday

The guests

The cake

The gifts

My favorite gift

Memories of the party

_____

_____

_____

_____

_____

_____

_____

_____

_____

_____

_____

My photos

The first time that

I stopped wearing diapers

_____

_____

I drew a circle

_____

_____

I recognized colors

_____

_____

I counted up to 5

_____

_____

I brushed my teeth myself

_____

_____

I rode a tricycle _____

_____

I dressed on my own _____

_____

I used my own name _____

_____

A new experience _____

_____

_____

_____

My friends

My friends are called

These are the games I play with them

My favorites

My favorite book

_____

The toy I never get bored with

_____

I smile every time I hear this song

_____

I like playing these games with Mom and Dad

_____

The thing that makes me happier than anything else

_____

The thing that makes me angrier than anything else

_____

What consoles me

_____

A special occasion

The event

_____

_____

_____

_____

Who was there

_____

_____

_____

How I behaved

_____

_____

_____

_____

An unforgettable memory

_____

_____

_____

_____

_____

_____

My third birthday

The guests

_____

_____

_____

_____

The cake

_____

_____

The gifts

_____

_____

_____

My favorite gift

_____

_____

_____

_____

Memories of the party

_____

_____

_____

_____

_____

_____

_____

_____

_____

_____

_____

_____

_____

My photos

The first time that

I drew a picture of an animal

I went to a friend's party

I chose my clothes in the morning

I wrote my own name

I stopped using a pacifier

My photos

PROJECT EDITOR

Valeria Manferto De Fabianis

GRAPHIC DESIGN

Marinella Debernardi

PHOTO CREDITS

Cover: Mandrixta/iStockphoto; back cover: boboling/iStockphoto; ananaline/iStockphoto: pages 1, 4, 6 top right, 22, 29, 40, 45, 56; artisteer/iStockphoto: pages 66, 67; Boboling/iStockphoto: pages 47, 71; deyangeorgiev/iStockphoto: page 2; gralu87/iStockphoto: page 3; inurbanspace/iStockphoto: page 69; Izabelite/iStockphoto: pages 10, 14, 15, 20, 21, 24, 30, 31, 36, 37, 42, 48, 49, 60, 61, 78; joel-t/iStockphoto: page 68; Bobo Ling/123RF: pages 23, 41; Markus Mainka/123RF: pages 58, 59; Mandrixta/iStockphoto: pages 19, 44, 55, 57, 76, 77, 80; Moji1980/iStockphoto: page 38; Oz_Media/iStockphoto: page 12; Phuchong Choksamai/123RF: pages 50, 51, 52, 53, 62, 63, 64, 65, 72, 73, 74, 75; Marina Scurupii/123RF: pages 5, 6 bottom, 7, 8, 9, 13, 17, 27, 32, 33, 34, 35, 54; Tetiana Vitsenko/123RF: page 16

WS White Star Publishers® is a registered trademark property of De Agostini Libri S.p.A.

© 2016 De Agostini Libri S.p.A.

Via G. da Verrazano, 15 - 28100 Novara, Italy - www.whitestar.it - www.deagostini.it

ISBN 978-88-544-1071-8

1 2 3 4 5 6   20 19 18 17 16

Printed in China